Plants Make Babies Happy

by Jannell Joosse
Illustration by JuliaDreamsCo and AnneIllustration
Design by Jannell Joosse
ISBN: 9798480535792
Independently Published

Baby's First Book of

Plants

By Jannell Joosse

Sago Palm

Rubber Tree

Dracaena

Jade Plant

Plant kindness, little one.

Snake Plant

Peace Lily

Palm

English Ivy

Spider Plant

Plant love, little one.

Succulent

String of Pearls

Yucca

Fiddle Leaf Fig

Monstera

Plant your dreams, little one.

Watch
them grow.

Cactus

Aloe

The world has big plans for you, little one.

16989093R00017